tiny tabletop
gardens

tiny tabletop
gardens

35 projects for super-small
spaces—outdoors and in

EMMA HARDY

CICO BOOKS
LONDON · NEW YORK

Published in 2017 by CICO Books
An imprint of Ryland Peters & Small Ltd
20–21 Jockey's Fields, London WC1R 4BW
341 E 116th St, New York, NY 10029

www.rylandpeters.com

10 9 8 7 6 5 4 3 2 1

A CIP catalog record for this book is available from
the Library of Congress and the British Library.

ISBN: 978-1-78249-413-3

Printed in China

Editor: Caroline West
Designer: Luana Gobbo
Photographer: Debbie Patterson
Stylist: Emma Hardy

In-house editor: Anna Galkina
Art director: Sally Powell
Production controller: David Hearn
Publishing manager: Penny Craig
Publisher: Cindy Richards

~ contents

introduction

Gardening is one of life's great pleasures. The physical acts of digging, weeding, planting, and looking after plants are hugely satisfying. Being able to sit back and enjoy what develops and grows is also a real treat. If you are not lucky enough to have a garden or any outside space, don't let that put you off. Here are 35 small-scale projects divided up into plants suitable for growing indoors, containers for outdoors, and edible planting, as well as those that are perfect for a small tabletop, either for a balcony or patio, or perhaps for a special occasion.

Each project provides a list of all the tools and materials you will need, as well as a selection of recommended plants. You can stick closely to these lists, especially if you are a novice gardener, or simply use them for inspiration, adding your own ideas and using plants available to you to create planters and plant combinations you love. There are step-by-step instructions on how to put the gardens together, with tips for aftercare and maintenance once your teeny-tiny gardens are established.

It is a good idea to read the *Materials and Techniques* section (see pages 8–11) before you embark on a project, since it will help you choose containers, buy healthy plants, and decide on the most suitable potting mix to use. Most of the containers used in this book are old and were discovered in secondhand stores and markets—I like to use things that look as if they have a bit of history. Old pails (buckets), enamel dishes, and vintage cans (tins) all help to enhance the look of the plants, so keep your eyes open for interesting secondhand finds. If you are new to gardening, then look at the list of useful tools and equipment on page 11 and invest in a basic gardening kit, if you can, which will prove useful for all the projects in the book. Buy the best-quality tools you can afford and look after them well, cleaning them after use and storing them in a dry place—if you do this, they should last you for many years to come.

One of the most wonderful things about gardening is the sheer number of plants that are available, whether from local garden centers or online. I love playing with different color combinations, mixing textures and shapes, and combining foliage and flowers to make little gardens that look beautiful and bring pleasure to all who see them. I hope you will look at and enjoy the projects in this book and feel inspired to create your own container gardens, whatever their size or scale.

materials and techniques

One of the joys of gardening on a small scale is that you do not need lots of special techniques or a large arsenal of tools and materials to achieve success and gain great pleasure from the beauty of plants.

Choosing and preparing containers

Visit your local garden center and you will probably see a huge range of pots, window boxes, and tubs made from all sorts of materials and in a wide range of colors and sizes. While such places are often a good place to buy basic terracotta and ceramic pots, looking further afield will often provide you with far more interesting and unusual planters. Try secondhand sales and junk stores for old pails (buckets), tubs, and boxes that would look beautiful planted up. Old cans (tins) are especially useful, because it is easy to make drainage holes in the bottoms and they are also often available in bright, colorful designs.

An important factor when choosing a container for planting is whether it has at least one drainage hole in the base or if it is possible to make some. If not—and you really love the container—then consider using it for indoor planting or in a shaded area (such as a porch or balcony), where the watering can be controlled to avoid overwatering.

Preparing containers

It is important to clean any container you are using to reduce the risk of pests and diseases infecting your new plants. Scrub the container with warm soapy water, rinse thoroughly, and allow it to dry before you begin.

Making drainage holes

You will need to provide adequate drainage for the plants in your containers, so that the potting mix does not become waterlogged. Most plants do not like sitting in very wet soil, and making a few holes in the bottom of containers made from metal or wood, for example, with a hammer and sturdy nail will allow excess water to drain away.

Adding drainage crocks

Once your container has drainage holes, it is a good idea to cover these loosely with a few pieces of broken terracotta pot, old tiles, or old china (often referred to as "crocks"). This will help prevent the drainage holes becoming blocked with potting mix. Carefully smash up these old pots, tiles, or china with a hammer—it is a good idea to wear glasses or protective goggles when doing this—and place a few pieces in the bottom of the container. I find it useful to have a stash of these to hand for future projects.

Choosing and preparing plants

When planting up containers, choosing healthy plants is very important. Check that the plants are suitable for the size of container you are using, as a lack of space for root growth will produce unhappy plants. When gardening on a small scale, look for alpine plants, succulents, and dwarf varieties, which will all live happily in small containers. If you can, carefully remove the plant from its pot and check that it is not pot-bound and is also pest- and disease-free. Check the leaves and flowers are in good condition too.

Loosening the roots

If your plant is a little pot-bound and looks as if it has been in its pot a little too long, loosen the roots to encourage them to grow and spread out when planted up. Gently tease out the roots with your fingers, pulling them apart slightly, while being careful not to damage them too much.

Soaking plants

It is recommended that you soak the rootballs of plants before they are re-potted to give them the best possible start in their new container. Soak them in a pail (bucket) or tub of water for at least 10 minutes (longer for larger plants), or until they are soaked through.

Potting mixes

Your local garden center will stock a selection of potting mixes. This can seem overwhelming at first, especially to the beginner, so here is a simple guide to help you choose the correct one for the job. There are two main types of mix: soil-based potting mix and soil-less potting mix (which contains peat or a peat substitute).

Soil-based potting mix

This is a good, multi-purpose mix that is suitable for most of the projects in this book (unless specified otherwise). It is nutrient-rich and so will help new plants to establish well for the first six to eight weeks (after which feeding is recommended). It is also free-draining and encourages root growth. It is sold in various mixes with increasing levels of nutrients to suit the needs of different plants, as follows:

* Seed potting mixes provide a sterile growing medium that is low in nutrients to give seedlings the best start in life. Seedlings will need potting on to larger pots as they grow and require more nutrients.

* General-purpose potting mix is suitable for most plants grown in containers. The high nutrient levels will provide plants with all they need for root and foliar growth.

* Permanent plantings require a long-term potting mix that is nutrient-rich with slow-release fertilizers and will also provide adequate drainage.

Soil-less potting mix

This is lighter and often cheaper than soil-based alternatives, but is very free-draining and dries out very quickly—this can be a problem for containers, especially in warm weather. Soil-less potting mixes are perfectly good for short-term plantings, although you will need to feed the containers regularly with a liquid feed because they tend to be low in nutrients. They are not recommended for longer-term tubs and containers, where a soil-based potting mix will give much better results. Always avoid potting mixes that contain peat, the use of which is environmentally unfriendly.

Specialist potting mixes

Certain types of plant require specific growing conditions if they are to thrive. You can buy potting mixes that are specially formulated for these plants:

* Cactus and succulent mixes contain added grit to make them free-draining, and can often be purchased in small quantities. If you can't get hold of any, a general, multi-purpose potting mix will be fine. Add a little gravel or horticultural grit, if you have any.

* Ericaceous potting mix is suitable for lime-hating plants (see *Blueberries in a Tub*, on pages 84–87) and has a pH of below 7. Again, it is often available in smaller bags, making it suitable for planting up small containers.

Using additives

Potting mix in containers can benefit from several additives. Horticultural grit or sand and fine gravel can all help to improve drainage and prevent the potting mix from becoming waterlogged. Use finer grades for smaller plants, so that roots will not be damaged. Vermiculite (an expanded mineral) and perlite (a lightweight volcanic glass) are both available from garden centers and will help to lighten the potting mix and improve drainage and aeration. Additives are not essential, but can be very useful in container gardening.

Using additives

Mulches and decorative trims

A mulch is a dressing that covers the surface of the potting mix to help conserve moisture and act as a decorative trim. Gravel works well around succulents and cacti, as it not only helps to keep damp potting mix away from the leaves but also adds an attractive finish. Look for fine gravel, which is often available in different colors, or try using small or crushed shells, sand, broken glass, or small pebbles. Remember you are not allowed to remove shells or pebbles from beaches. Cushion moss can also be used as a decorative trim and makes containers look nice and lush.

Care and maintenance

Developing a regular maintenance routine for your container plants will ensure they flourish and provide you with lots of pleasure. Specific aftercare advice is given with individual projects, but below is some general guidance on caring for your plants:

Watering

The watering of plants grown in containers is very important, as they can dry out much faster than plants grown in the ground, especially in warm weather. Checking your plants regularly, and watering them if necessary, is vital if you want to keep your pots and tubs looking good, particularly during the growing season.

Most plants do not like sitting in soaking-wet potting mix and prefer a just-moist potting medium that is never allowed to get very dry. In the summer, check your containers daily and water if necessary. Ideally, water in the evening so that the sun does not cause too much evaporation, although if your plants look wilted at any time of the day, they will enjoy an additional watering. If you are going away for a few days, your plants will benefit from being moved to a shadier spot, which will help them to retain moisture. Give them a good watering just before you leave, too.

Water-retaining granules can be a useful addition to potting mix, especially in small containers that dry out particularly quickly. Simply mix them into the potting medium before planting.

Indoor plants require more careful watering, as their containers often don't have drainage holes and so can easily be overwatered. Check the potting mix weekly and water if need be, avoiding letting plants sit in too much water. Houseplants, terrariums, and air plants require a weekly misting with a water spray bottle. Cacti and succulents cope very well with drying out, although they will be happier in a potting mix that is kept just moist, but is never very wet.

Feeding

General-purpose potting mixes provide plants with enough nutrients for the first six to eight weeks after planting. After that, container-grown plants will benefit from additional feeding, either with a liquid feed or with slow-release fertilizer granules that can be mixed into the potting mix.

* Liquid feeds are available in a range of mixes suitable for specific plants and their requirements. A reputable, general, multi-purpose liquid feed is a good buy and will be suitable for most outdoor containers. Follow the manufacturer's instructions for diluting the feed and use either weekly or fortnightly throughout the growing season. Specific feeds (for tomatoes or indoor plants, for example) can also be useful.

* Slow-release fertilizer granules can be added to the potting mix before planting or forked into the top of the potting mix in established containers to reduce the need for regular liquid feeds.

* A foliar feed is a diluted feed that can be sprayed directly onto plants, providing them with an instant boost. This is useful for a one-off pick-me-up, but should not be used instead of applying fertilizers to the potting mix, which will help to keep your plants healthy. Spray plants out of direct sunlight to avoid damaging their leaves.

Deadheading

Removing dead flower heads and leaves from plants helps to encourage new growth, often increasing flowering as well as keeping plants tidy. Deadheading plants regularly will encourage them to put their energy into new growth, instead of setting seed, which means that the flowering season will last much longer. For plants with soft stems,

Deadheading flowers

simply remove the dead flowers with your fingertips; use scissors or hand pruners (secateurs) for plants with tougher stems. Deadheading can also help to reduce the incidence of pests and diseases that may accumulate in dead plant matter.

Pests and diseases

Pests and diseases can quickly take hold of plants and so it is worth being vigilant with your containers. Act quickly if problems arise to ensure your container plantings look good and stay healthy for longer. Follow these simple rules and your plants will bloom:

* Always clean containers thoroughly before planting.

* Buy plants that look strong, have a healthy rootball which is not pot-bound, and show no obvious signs of pests or diseases.

* Invest in a good-quality potting mix, thinking about its suitability for the plants you are using.

* Monitor plants to ensure that you spot any problems quickly and so that any signs of pest infestation can be resolved quickly.

* Feed your plants regularly, as the healthier they are, the less likely they are to succumb to problems.

Aphids (greenfly and blackfly) are common pests that suck the sap from plants and can cause a lot of damage. If you spot only a few, then removing them with your fingers as and when you see them should keep them under control. For heavier infestations, spray your plants with a diluted mixture of dish-washing detergent and water. Commercial products are available, but I am not keen on using chemicals in the garden.

Botrytis (gray mold) is a fungal infection and can be seen as a whitish powder on foliage. It thrives in damp areas where the ventilation is poor. Improve ventilation and use an organic fungicide if necessary. Sometimes foliage can develop a whitish bloom when a plant is very dry, but additional watering and feeding should remedy this.

TIP: If pests or diseases have taken a firm hold, and you would like to use a commercially produced treatment, look for organic products if possible. This will result in healthier plants and won't harm more welcome wildlife, which can help to reduce pest infestations naturally.

USEFUL TOOLS AND EQUIPMENT

Here are some suggestions for a basic gardening kit, which will be useful for all the projects in this book. Invest in the best tools you can afford, look after them well, and they should last a long time.

Garden trowel

Garden fork

Metal spoons

Gardening gloves

Hammer and heavy-duty nail (for putting drainage holes in containers)

Hand pruners (secateurs)

Scissors

Garden string

Plant labels

Small watering can (with a fine rose)

Water spray bottle

Chapter 1
INDOORS

AFTERCARE

Succulent plants such
as crassulas, sempervivums,
and haworthias prefer dry
growing conditions, so do not
overwater them: allow the
potting mix to dry out
between waterings.

bright cans with indoor plants

This is a great idea for recycling empty food cans (tins)—choose cans with bright and colorful labels for maximum impact. Displaying the cans in a group with a selection of small plants suitable for growing indoors creates a lively and unusual focal point.

YOU WILL NEED

Old food cans (tins) with colorful labels

Hammer and heavy-duty nail

Gravel

Potting mix

Plants (in the cans only):

TOP SHELF (FROM LEFT TO RIGHT):
Sedum 'Matrona' (stonecrop),
Crassula ovata 'Gollum,'
Begonia Beleaf, and
Haworthia cooperi

LOWER SHELF (FROM LEFT TO RIGHT):
Portulacaria afra 'Variegata' (rainbow bush), *Sempervivum erythraeum* (houseleek), *Crassula ovata* 'Variegata' (friendship tree), and *Haworthia attenuata* var. *radula*

1 Wash the cans (tins) in soapy water, then rinse and dry them thoroughly. Turn each can upside down and punch a few holes in the base using the nail and hammer to make drainage holes. If you are displaying the plants in an area that needs to remain dry, either place small saucers under each can or leave the cans without drainage holes, making sure you do not overwater them.

2 Add a few handfuls of gravel to the bottom of the can to help with drainage, and level off.

3 Half-fill the can with potting mix and level the surface again.

4 Take the first plant out of its pot and carefully remove a little of the potting mix to ensure it will fit easily into the can. Place the plant in the can so the upper surface of the plant's rootball sits just under the rim. Add a little more potting mix, if necessary, to fill in any gaps and press down the surface slightly. Repeat for the remaining cans. Water the potting mix, ensuring that it is not soaking wet.

1

2

3

4

tiny glass jar terrariums

Terrariums really can be tiny, and these charming little glass jars are perfect for the job. I was lucky enough to find some jars with open, wire-topped lids that look great and also provide ventilation for the plants. If you can't find any like these, look for conserving jars, which often have a loose disk for a lid that can be removed, or simply remove the lid every now and then and check that the plants you are using are happy in more humid conditions.

YOU WILL NEED

Glass jars with screw-top lids

Fine gravel

Ground charcoal (if using sealed jars; available from pet stores)

Small spoon

Potting mix (with a little sand or vermiculite added)

Decorative sand (optional)

Paintbrush

Small shells, pebbles, or small stones, for decoration

Water spray bottle, for misting the plants

Plants:

FRONT JAR: *Aloe juvenna* (tiger tooth aloe)

RIGHT JAR: *Sedum* × *rubrotinctum* (banana cactus)

BACK JAR: *Fittonia albivensis* Argyroneura Group (nerve plant)

AFTERCARE

If your jars are completely
sealed, remember to remove
the lids from time to time in
order to air the plants.

1

2

3

4

5

6

7

8

9

1 Wash the jar and dry it thoroughly before you start. Put a couple of handfuls of fine gravel in the bottom of the jar, pouring it in gradually so that the glass does not crack. If you are using a jar with no ventilation, then it is a good idea to add a thin layer of ground charcoal at this stage too, to help reduce odors. This won't be necessary if the jar you are using is open-topped.

2 Using the spoon, add potting mix to the bottom of the jar to cover the gravel. Hold the jar upright so that the gravel stays in a flat layer.

3 Take the first plant out of its pot and carefully remove some of the potting mix from around the roots, taking care not to damage them.

4 Push the plant, roots first, into the jar and settle it onto the potting mix, holding it in place with your fingers (or a spoon if the jar is too small).

5 Add potting mix around the base of the plant, covering the roots. Push the potting mix down with the back of the spoon, so that the plant is held firmly in place. Try not to add too much potting mix, or it will create a large, dark stripe in your terrarium.

6 Wipe the spoon clean. Spoon more gravel or some decorative sand onto the layer of potting mix, again pressing it down to remove any air pockets and create an even layer.

7 Gently brush off the gravel or sand from the plant using the paintbrush. Brush the inside of the jar as well to clean it, if necessary. Plant the other glass jars in the same way.

8 Add a few decorative shells to the gravel or sand surface, if you wish, or try using a few pebbles or small stones instead.

9 Use the spray bottle to water the glass terrariums sparingly, making sure the potting mix does not get too wet. Put the lid on each jar.

AFTERCARE

Remove the plants twice a week in warm weather, less often in colder months, and soak them in water, as in Step 1. If the leaves start to curl, the plants may be dehydrated. Soak them overnight to revive them.

air plants on wood

Tillandsias are intriguing plants that I have only recently discovered. Classed as air plants, they do not need a growing medium and require very little attention apart from regular watering. Although tillandsias need plenty of natural light, they will not thrive in direct sunlight. Provide humid conditions with good air circulation, and they will be happy.

YOU WILL NEED

Shallow bowl

Piece of bark or a tree stump

Water spray bottle

A selection of tillandsias:

Tillandsia andreana,
T. baileyi, *T. bulbosa*,
T. fuchsii var. *gracilis*, and
T. tricolor var. *melanocrater*

1 Fill a shallow bowl with water (ideally, rainwater should be used, but tap water is fine too). Soak the air plants in the water, submerging them completely, and leave for a few minutes. Take out the plants and allow them to drain.

2 Place the piece of bark on a table and look for holes, nooks, and crannies that the plants can sit in. Carefully push the first air plant into a hole, making sure you do not damage it. Continue pushing the other air plants into the bark, varying the colors and textures of the plants that are placed next to each other.

3 Mist the air plants with the spray bottle every few days to help create humid conditions.

water plants in glass jars

You can enjoy water plants without the need for a pond or aquarium. Choose a few glass jars in different sizes and add sand, gravel, shells, and pebbles, plus one or two water plants to each one, to create an unusual tabletop garden. Plants for home aquariums are ideal, as they are usually quite small. They are also more suitable than pond plants, which will probably be too large for these jars.

YOU WILL NEED

Glass jars

Aquatic sand (available from pet stores and garden centers)

Spoon

Shells and pebbles

Aquatic gravel (available from pet stores and garden centers)

Tap water that has been left in an open container for a day or two in order to allow chemicals such as chlorine to evaporate

A selection of water plants, such as:

Aponogeton ulvaceus (compact aponogeton)

Echinodorus bleheri (Amazon sword)

Echinodorus 'Ozelot' (ozelot sword)

AFTERCARE

Keep the jars out of direct sunlight to help reduce the growth of algae inside. When the water levels drop, use an old toothbrush or cloth to remove any algae from the inside of the jars, before filling them with more water.

1 Make sure that the jars are clean and dry before you start. Pour a few inches of sand into the bottom of each jar.

2 Take one of the plants and place it in the first jar, burying the roots in the sand. A spoon will prove helpful here if the jar is too small for you to get both hands inside.

3 If you wish, you can add another plant to the jar, although there may not be enough room if the first plant is large.

4 Add a selection of shells and pebbles to decorate the jar, laying them carefully on the sand. Note: you are not allowed to remove pebbles or shells from beaches, but they can usually be purchased from garden-supply stores.

5 Alternatively, you can add a layer of gravel to the surface of the sand, being careful not to damage the plants as you pour it in. Try to level off the gravel so that it forms an even layer.

6 Plant the remaining jars in the same way. Fill each jar with the water, pouring it slowly over the back of the spoon so that it doesn't disturb the sand and/ or gravel. Leave the jars to rest—the water may look bubbly and cloudy at first, but will clear in a few hours.

japanese moss balls

Traditionally called *kokedama*, these Japanese moss balls are easy to make and a stunning way to display and grow indoor plants. Sheet moss is used to create a ball around the plant's roots, which keeps the plant looking beautiful and healthy for a long time if it is watered and maintained well. Place the moss balls on dishes to protect surfaces from moisture. You can also suspend the balls with nylon thread, but check they can be easily reached for watering.

1 Take the plant from its pot and very gently remove any excess potting mix, being careful not to damage the roots.

2 Mix two-thirds potting mix with one-third bonsai potting mix—to give the correct level of moisture retention and drainage. If you have any sphagnum moss, then a few pieces can also be added to help retain moisture, although this is not essential. Add some water to the combined potting mix to make it very wet.

YOU WILL NEED

Potting mix

Bonsai potting mix

Sphagnum moss (optional)

Sheet moss (available from garden centers and florists)

Fine nylon thread (available from anglers' shops)

Scissors

Plants:

Phalaenopsis (moth orchid)

Polystichum braunii (Braun's holly fern)

3 Put handfuls of wet potting mix around the plant's roots, squeezing as you go to create a ball that holds its shape well. Carefully squeeze out the excess water.

4 Lay a sheet of moss, with the upper side facing down, on the work surface. Place the ball of potting mix on top of the moss sheet and pull the moss over to cover it.

5 Cut away any excess moss so that it forms a neat covering around the potting-mix ball. Moss is very forgiving and so it is easy to create a neat finish.

6 Tie some nylon thread around the moss ball and secure with a firm knot. Continue to wrap the thread around the ball, being careful not to damage the plant, until the moss forms a nice round shape and will not fall off. Finish with a knot in the thread and trim the ends neatly. Water the moss ball and allow to drain well.

AFTERCARE

Orchids prefer a warm,
sheltered spot out of direct
sunlight. Water regularly, ensuring
that the roots do not dry out
completely, but allow the moss
ball to drain, as orchids do not
like to sit in water.

cactus and succulent garden

This charming cactus and succulent garden is very easy to make and requires little maintenance, making it the perfect teeny-tiny garden if you do not have much space. Make sure the planter does not sit on a surface such as a table that may be damaged by water, or place it on a small tray to provide protection.

YOU WILL NEED

Old, rectangular, metal cake pan (tin) or similar

Hammer and heavy-duty nail

Drainage crocks

Potting mix (with a little sand or vermiculite added to help with drainage)

Fine gravel

Plants:

Cleistocactus strausii (silver torch)

Crassula muscosa (moss cypress)

Euphorbia trigona (marble column)

Haworthia cooperi

Kalanchoe thyrsiflora (paddle plant)

Portulacaria afra 'Variegata' (rainbow bush)

Sansevieria 'Fernwood' (snake plant)

Sedum burrito (burro's tail)

Sedum spurium 'Fuldaglut' (Caucasian stonecrop)

Sempervivum erythraeum, *S.* 'Fuego,' and *S.* 'Springmist' (houseleek)

1 The pan (tin) will need good drainage, so, if it does not already have holes in the base, make some randomly using the hammer and nail.

2 Cover the holes with drainage crocks, so that they will not become blocked with potting mix.

3 Half-fill the pan (tin) with potting mix and level the surface.

4 Take the plants out of their pots and start to arrange them in the pan (tin), moving them around carefully (especially if they are spiky!) until you are happy with the arrangement. In general, using the taller plants toward the back with the smaller ones at the front works well, but play around with the design, varying the colors and shapes of the plants that sit next to each other.

5 Add potting mix around the plants, making sure that there are no air pockets and filling in any gaps. Level the surface of the potting mix.

6 Add some gravel to the surface of the potting mix, ensuring that it does not damage the more delicate plants. Water the pan (tin) and leave to drain.

AFTERCARE

Cacti and succulents are largely maintenance-free, but still need occasional watering, ideally using tepid rainwater as the minerals in tap water can accumulate in the potting mix and leave deposits on the leaves.

AFTERCARE

Succulents do not need much
water and will not like sitting
in very wet potting mix.
So, it's important to check the
plants from time to time and
water if necessary, but make
sure you don't overwater.

shells with succulents

Succulents are ideal for this type of planting because they root easily and require simple growing conditions. Their shapes and colors also work well with the organic forms of the shells. Try different plants together to create interesting arrangements.

YOU WILL NEED

Large shells

Specialist potting mix (suitable for cacti and succulents)

A selection of succulents, such as:

Aeonium arboreum 'Atropurpureum' (dark purple houseleek tree)

Aloe juvenna (tiger tooth aloe)

Cotyledon papillaris

Echeveria 'Purple Pearl'

Pachyphytum glutinicaule

Sedum album (white stonecrop), *S. nussbaumerianum* (stonecrop), *S. × rubrotinctum* (banana cactus), and *S. stahlii* (coral beads)

Sempervivum erythraeum (houseleek)

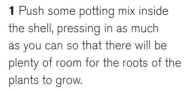

1 Push some potting mix inside the shell, pressing in as much as you can so that there will be plenty of room for the roots of the plants to grow.

2 Soak the plants' roots in water for a few minutes and then remove the plants from their pots. Carefully loosen the potting mix around the roots of the largest plant and push the plant into the potting mix in the shell.

3 Take the second plant and again remove some of the potting mix from around the roots. Push the roots into the shell so that the plant is held firmly in place.

4 Take the last plant and, having loosened the potting mix as before, tuck the roots between the first two plants, using your little finger or the blunt end of a pencil to ensure the roots are completely planted in the potting mix. Plant up the other shells, water carefully, and leave to drain. You can display the shells outdoors if the succulents you have chosen are hardy; otherwise, keep them indoors to enjoy.

orchid and fern dome

Create an elegant indoor garden using a stylish glass dome planted with a beautiful orchid and delicate fern. Make sure you choose a little moth orchid that has a small rootball. Lush pieces of pincushion moss complete the look—the moss should retain its beautiful color if it is kept damp. If you can't get hold of cushion moss, try flower markets or ask a local florist to order some for you. Otherwise, sheet moss will work just as well.

YOU WILL NEED

Glass dome with a waterproof base

Fine gravel

Ground charcoal (available from pet stores)

Potting mix

Large pebble (optional)

Water spray bottle

Plants:

Asparagus densiflorus Sprengeri Group (emerald feather)

Leucobryum albidum (pincushion moss)

Phalaenopsis (moth orchid)

1 The base of the dome needs to be waterproof, so that it will not be damaged by moisture. (If the base is made from wood, line it first with a disk of plastic sheeting or a small saucer.) Put a layer of gravel over the base and spread it out evenly.

AFTERCARE

The plants will sit happily
inside the glass dome, but it
is a good idea to remove the top
every few days to check the moisture
levels, spraying the moss
if it is very dry.

2 Sprinkle some ground charcoal over the gravel, to help absorb unpleasant odors from the potting mix and moss.

3 Put a layer of potting mix over the gravel and charcoal, piling it up a little in the middle.

4 Take the orchid from its plastic pot and carefully remove any excess growing medium from the roots. Tuck the roots into the potting mix and press the mix around the plant to hold it in place.

5 Break off a small piece of the fern by pulling the roots apart. Choose a small section from the edge of the plant and try to handle the roots carefully.

6 Plant the piece of fern in the potting mix, again pressing around the roots so that it is held firmly in place. Use a large pebble to help hold the roots in place if necessary.

7 Take a few pieces of moss and place them around the plants, pressing them into the potting mix to form a neat dome. Mist the plants with the water spray bottle and place the glass dome over the top.

small urns
with succulents

I found these sweet little urns in a flower market and couldn't resist them. They make perfect containers for a little collection of succulents, which don't need a lot of room for root growth and require minimal watering—this means that they don't need much drainage. For each urn, choose three or four plants with different colors and textures, adding some gravel to cover the potting mix.

YOU WILL NEED

Small decorative urns or similar

Fine gravel

Potting mix

Plants:

Crassula arborescens subsp. *undulatifolia* (silver jade plant)

Crassula ovata (friendship tree)

Echeveria 'Purple Pearl'

Sedeveria 'Blue Giant'

Sedum stahlii (coral beads)

Sempervivum 'Ohio Burgundy' (houseleek)

Senecio rowleyanus (string of beads)

1 Sprinkle a handful of gravel into the bottom of each urn.

AFTERCARE

Water the plants sparingly, if necessary, but make sure that you do not overwater them. Position the urns in a light spot.

2 Add some potting mix to the urns, blending it into the gravel a little to prevent the potting mix from becoming too compacted after watering.

3 The potting mix around the plants' roots should be damp, but not too wet, so soak the plants in water for just a few minutes and then allow them to drain before you start planting. Take the first succulent from its pot (it doesn't matter in which order you plant them), gently scrape away excess potting mix, and plant in the first urn.

4 Add the remaining plants to the urn in the same way, removing excess potting mix so that the plants all fit inside.

5 Firm in the potting mix around the plants with your fingertips, so that they sit securely in place.

6 Add a little more potting mix around the plants, if necessary, to fill in any gaps. Level the surface and brush any bits of potting mix from the plants. Plant up the other urn in the same way.

7 Sprinkle gravel onto the surface of the potting mix in the urns. This not only looks good, but also helps to conserve water. Again, remove any stray gravel from the plants. The plants may not need watering immediately, so leave the urns for a few days, check the potting mix, and then water if necessary.

indoor plants in cream pots

Grouping together a collection of houseplants can create real impact in a room. Look for plants with a variety of colors, textures, and leaf sizes, uniting them in pots of a similar color or finish. Choose pots that are not much bigger than the rootballs of your plants—unless you want them to grow a lot larger—because otherwise they will end up sitting in lots of wet potting mix.

YOU WILL NEED

Selection of pots in pale colors

Drainage crocks

Potting mix

Water spray bottle, for misting the plants

Plants (from left to right):

Phlebodium aureum 'Blue Star' (rabbit's foot fern)

Philodendron xanadu

Aloe vera (Barbados aloe)

Maranta leuconeura (prayer plant)

Echinopsis lageniformis (Bolivian torch cactus)

Calathea roseopicta 'Medallion' (zebra plant)

Fatsia japonica (Japanese aralia)

1 If any of the pots have drainage holes, then put a few drainage crocks in the bottom so that they do not become blocked with wet potting mix.

2 Add some potting mix to the first pot and level the surface. Don't add too much potting mix at this stage.

3 Take the first plant out of the plastic pot and place it in its ornamental pot. The surface of the plant's rootball should sit an inch or so under the rim, so add or take away potting mix from the bottom of the pot as necessary.

4 Fill around the rootball with more potting mix, pushing it down the sides of the pot so that there are no air pockets. Plant the remaining pots in the same way. Water the plants and leave to drain.

5 Houseplants enjoy being misted from time to time, so mist their leaves with a water spray bottle in order to keep them healthy.

1

2

3

4

5

AFTERCARE

Check the potting mix regularly
and water when necessary,
making sure that the pots are
not overwatered if there
are no drainage holes
in the bottom.

Chapter 2
OUTDOORS

planted enamel ladles

This lovely little display uses simple enamel ladles planted with pretty succulents to create a really charming result. Choose ladles with a large cup so that the roots of the plants will have enough room to grow and spread. Break off pieces from the larger succulents—these are generally quite tough plants and can take a bit of rough handling—and firm them into the potting mix well so they can take root and thrive.

YOU WILL NEED

Enamel ladles

Potting mix

Handful of gravel

Plants:

Left ladle: Moss (available from garden centers and florists)

Middle ladle: *Echeveria* 'Perle von Nürnberg,' *Sedum album* (white stonecrop), *S. burrito* (burro's tail), *S.* × *rubrotinctum* (banana cactus), and *Sempervivum* 'Ohio Burgundy' (houseleek)

Right ladle: *Anacampseros telephiastrum*, *Crassula ovata* (friendship tree), and *Sedum spathulifolium* 'Cape Blanco' (stonecrop)

1 Soak the rootballs of the plants for 10 minutes or so until the potting mix is wet. Put a handful of potting mix in the bottom of the ladle and add a little gravel to improve drainage.

2 Carefully take one of the larger succulents from its pot and remove some of the excess potting mix to reduce the size of the rootball. Plant it on one side of the ladle.

3 Take another of the larger succulents from its pot and again remove some of the potting mix. Plant at the back of the ladle, firming it in place.

4 Add the smaller succulents to the ladle, breaking smaller bits off the larger plants if necessary, and plant them around the larger ones. Press down the potting mix.

5 Fill in any holes with more potting mix and firm it in place so that the plants will not move.

6 Add a sprinkling of gravel to the surface of the potting mix, pushing it around the plants with your fingers. This will help keep moisture in and looks nice, too. Plant up the other ladles and then water carefully, allowing excess water to drain off.

AFTERCARE

Succulents can withstand dry conditions, but remember to check the potting mix regularly and water the ladles when they are very dry.

metal container with white flowers

This lovely old metal container looks stunning planted with simple white flowers. Mixing flowers of the same color, but in different sizes, makes for an interesting look. Here, the white cosmos, with their large petals; the petunias and violas, with their smaller blooms; and the delicate flowers of the euphorbia all work well together.

YOU WILL NEED

Deep metal container

Hammer and heavy-duty nail (optional)

Drainage crocks

Potting mix

Plants:

Cosmos bipinnatus 'Sonata White'

Euphorbia hypericifolia 'Glitz'

Petunia multiflora 'Surprise White Improved'

Viola cornuta Alba Group (horned violet)

1 Soak the rootballs of all the plants in water for about half an hour. If the container does not have drainage holes, make some using the hammer and nail, positioning the holes randomly all over the base.

2 Cover the drainage holes in the bottom of the container with crocks, so that they will not become blocked with potting mix.

3 Half-fill the container with potting mix and level the surface.

4 Take the viola from its plastic pot, loosen the roots slightly, and plant at the back of the box.

5 Remove the cosmos from its pot and plant it next to the viola. The tops of the plants' rootballs should sit about an inch below the top of the container.

6 Next, take the petunia and euphorbia from their pots and plant them at the front of the container. Add some more potting mix to fill in any gaps. Water the container.

AFTERCARE
Check the potting mix in warm weather and water the container if it dries out. Deadhead the plants regularly to keep them flowering.

metal tray with pansies and petunias

Create a striking table centerpiece by planting petunias with striking black violas and purple pansies. Add candles for a special occasion, using small metal cake pans (tins) or glass jars pushed into the potting mix as candleholders (just ensure the candles are positioned away from the leaves). This is definitely a display in which more is more and an ideal opportunity to create a dense-looking planter.

YOU WILL NEED

Old metal tray

Drainage crocks

Potting mix

Moss (available from garden centers and florists)

Candles and small candleholders (optional)

Plants:

4 *Hedera* (trailing ivy)

3 *Petunia* 'Black Mamba'

9 *Petunia* 'Trailing Cappuccino'

9 black *Viola*

3 purple *Viola* × *wittrockiana* (pansy)

1 Soak the rootballs of all the plants in water. Small plants will need only 5–10 minutes' soaking, but leave larger plants for longer. Ensure the tray has drainage holes in the base. (See page 8 for advice on adding holes.) Cover the holes with crocks so that they will not become blocked with potting mix, which will impede drainage.

2 Half-fill the tray with potting mix, spreading it out evenly and leveling the surface.

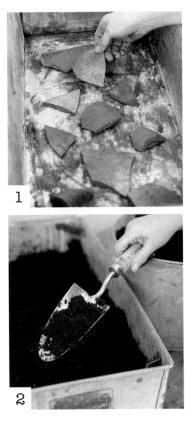

3 Remove the petunias from their plastic tray and dot them around the metal tray. Add or remove potting mix, as necessary, so that the surface of each plant's rootball sits below the rim of the tray.

4 Take the violas and pansies out of their trays and plant them around the petunias, packing them in so that the tray looks lovely and full.

5 Remove the ivies from their pots and plant them around the sides of the tray so that they trail over the edges.

6 Fill any gaps with more potting mix, making sure that there are no air pockets. Press down the surface of the potting mix firmly. Tear the moss into pieces and push these onto the surface of the potting mix to cover it. This adds a decorative touch and finishes the look of the tray beautifully. Water the tray. (If you add candles to the display, remember never to leave them unattended when they are lit.)

AFTERCARE

Check the potting mix regularly
to make sure it is moist, but not
too wet. Deadhead the plants
in order to prolong the
flowering period.

yellow tub with spring flowers

After a gloomy winter I can't wait to see beautiful spring flowers, and this pretty planter will definitely help to brush away the winter blues. The charming pale yellow enamel tub really sets off the colors of the plants, so look for a pastel-colored pot or tub and plant it with hyacinths, grape hyacinths, saxifrage, and violas, adding lush green moss to finish off the look.

YOU WILL NEED

Old enamel tub

Drainage crocks

Potting mix

Moss (available from garden centers and florists)

Plants:

2 or 3 *Hyacinthus orientalis* 'Blue Pearl' (hyacinth)

Muscari aucheri 'Blue Magic' and *M. azureum* 'Album' (grape hyacinth)

Saxifraga Alpino Early Pink Heart (saxifrage)

Deep purple and pale lilac *Viola*

1 Cover the holes in the base of the tub with a few drainage crocks to help with drainage. (See page 8 for guidance on adding holes if the tub does not have any.)

2 Half-fill the tub with potting mix and level the surface.

3 Take the hyacinths from their pots, removing any loose potting mix from around the bulbs. Place them in the tub and mound up the potting mix slightly to hold them in place.

4 Remove the grape hyacinths from their pots and plant them in the tub next, again using the surrounding potting mix to hold them in position.

5 Soak the rootballs of the remaining plants in water for 5–10 minutes. Gently remove the saxifrage from its pot and plant it near the edge of the tub.

6 Plant the violas in the tub, dotting them among the other plants to fill any gaps.

7 Add extra potting mix to fill between the plants, leveling the surface.

8 Finish off the arrangement with small pieces of moss to cover any areas of bare potting mix. Simply tear off pieces of moss and fit them neatly around the bases of the plants. Water the tub.

AFTERCARE

Check the tub regularly,
keeping the potting mix moist,
and deadhead the violas so they
will continue to produce flowers.
When the hyacinths have died off,
remove them and add more violas
so that the tub continues
to look fresh.

planted teapots and jugs

A collection of pretty teapots and jugs is a lovely way to display bedding plants. Old and vintage teapots and jugs can often be found cheaply at tabletop sales and secondhand markets, and provide a lovely decoration when planted for a summer party or gathering.

1 Soak the rootballs of the plants in water for at least half an hour. Wash the teapots and jugs in soapy water, then rinse and dry them thoroughly before you begin. Add a few handfuls of gravel to the bottom of each teapot and jug. As there are no drainage holes in these containers, it is important to add some gravel to help with drainage and prevent the potting mix from becoming a soggy, solid mass.

2 Put potting mix in the bottom of the teapot, mixing in a little vermiculite or perlite if you have any. This will help improve drainage and aeration.

3 Take the first plant—here, the diascia—from its plastic pot and gently remove some of the potting mix, trying not to damage the roots too much. This is especially important if the teapot or jug has a narrow neck.

4 Gently push the roots of the plant into the teapot, so that the top of the plant's rootball is sitting just below the rim. Add more potting mix to the bottom of the teapot if the plant is sitting too low. Plant up the other teapots and jugs with the remaining plants.

5 Water the plants sparingly so that the potting mix is damp, but not too wet.

metal trough with flowers and foliage

If you only have room for a window box, then make it a fabulous one! Forget planting a few bedding plants and instead choose some beautiful heuchera, heucherella, and tiarella, with their lovely feathery flowers, and add hostas for a foliage-rich display. Try to find a large, deep trough, so that there will be plenty of room for the roots to spread.

YOU WILL NEED
Metal trough
Hammer and heavy-duty nail
Drainage crocks
Potting mix

Plants:
Heuchera 'Cherry Cola' and *H*. 'Mahogany' (coral flower)

Heucherella 'Art Nouveau', *H*. 'Hot Spot', and *H*. 'Solar Power'

Hosta 'Guacamole' and *H*. 'Sherborne Swift' (plantain lily)

Tiarella 'Spring Symphony' (foam flower)

1 Soak the rootballs of the plants in water for about 20 minutes, or until they are completely soaked through. Use the hammer and nail to make holes in the base of the trough, if necessary, to help with drainage (see page 8 for guidance on adding holes in this way). Cover the base of the trough with drainage crocks to prevent the holes from becoming blocked with potting mix.

2 Half-fill the trough with potting mix and level the surface.

3 Take one of the hostas out of its pot and plant it in the trough, positioning it at one end.

4 Plant another plant next to the hosta and continue in this way until all the plants are in the trough. Add or take away potting mix, as required, so that the surfaces of all the plants' rootballs are level with each other.

5 Add handfuls of potting mix around the plants, making sure that there are no air pockets and filling in any gaps. Level the surface of the potting mix and water, allowing the trough to drain.

AFTERCARE

Feed the plants in the
container with a general-purpose
fertilizer every few weeks
(see page 10) throughout the
summer to keep them in
tip-top condition.

wooden box with orange flowers

This wooden box reminds me of a treasure chest, bursting open with a display of flowers in shades of orange and yellow. I didn't want to spoil my box, so I lined it with plastic sheeting to protect the wood and make sure it is never overwatered. If you are happy to add holes, then omit the first step and add plenty of crocks to help with drainage.

YOU WILL NEED

Old wooden box

Black plastic sheeting

Staple gun and staples

Potting mix

Plants:

Bidens Beedance Painted Yellow

Calibrachoa Can Can Series 'Apricot' and *C.* Volcano Sunrise (mini petunia)

Geum 'Totally Tangerine' (avens)

Osteospermum 'Sunny Fanny' (African daisy)

Papaver nudicale 'Spring Fever Orange' and *P. nudicale* 'Spring Fever Yellow' (Icelandic poppy)

6 orange *Viola* × *wittrockiana* (pansy)

1 Soak the rootballs of the plants in water for about 20 minutes, or until they are soaking wet. Line the inside of the box with the black plastic sheeting, folding it at the corners and stapling it into place all around the top.

2 Half-fill the box with potting mix and then level off the surface.

3 Take one of the tallest plants—in this case, the osteospermum—and plant it toward the back of the box.

4 Continue to plant the taller plants around this plant, adding or taking away potting mix, as required, so that the surfaces of all the plants' rootballs are level and sitting just under the rim of the box.

5 Add the smaller plants in the gaps between the larger ones, trailing some slightly over the edge.

6 Put a few handfuls of potting mix in the box to fill in any gaps, and level the surface. Water the potting mix, making sure that it is not too sodden.

AFTERCARE

Deadhead the flowers regularly
to encourage them to produce
further flushes of flowers.

vibrant vintage cans

Dahlias have such colorful flowers, but seemed to fall out of favor for a long time. However, I'm glad to say that they are back. These colorful vintage cans (tins) really bring out the vibrancy of the flowers and work both inside or out. Make sure you provide adequate drainage, as dahlias will not flower well if they are sitting in very wet potting mix.

YOU WILL NEED

Selection of vintage cans (tins)

Hammer and heavy-duty nail

Drainage crocks

Gravel

Potting mix

PLANTS:

Dahlia 'Amazone' and
D. Dahlietta Paula

1

2

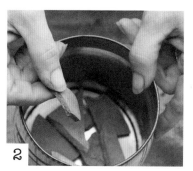

3

4

5

1 Soak the rootballs of the dahlias for half an hour or so. The cans (tins) will need drainage holes so that the potting mix does not become waterlogged. Use the hammer and sturdy nail to make holes in the bases of the cans.

2 Add drainage crocks to the bottom of the first can, covering the drainage holes so that they will not become blocked with potting mix.

3 Put a couple of handfuls of gravel in the bottom of the can, which will again help to improve drainage.

4 Half-fill the can with potting mix and level off, making sure that there are no air pockets. You can do this by gently tapping the can on the ground to help the potting mix settle.

5 Take the first plant from its pot and gently remove some of the potting mix, being careful not to damage the roots. Plant the dahlia in the can, adding more potting mix around the top so that it sits an inch or so below the rim. Repeat for the other cans and water sparingly.

AFTERCARE
Check the potting mix every few days in hot weather, keeping it moist but not too wet.

grass and flowers metal planter

Keeping the colors simple can result in a beautiful planting scheme. Adding grasses to this planter creates a delicate and stylish look that emulates the prairie planting that is very popular at the moment. The planter I used was covered with holes, so lining it with moss prevented the potting mix from falling out. Burlap (hessian) sacking could be used instead if you cannot get hold of enough moss.

YOU WILL NEED

Metal planter

Black plastic sheeting (optional)

Moss (available from florists and garden centers)

Potting mix

Plants:

Astrantia major 'Midnight Owl' (masterwort)

Centranthus ruber var. *coccineus* 'Rosenrot' (red valerian)

Deschampsia cespitosa (tufted hairgrass)

Digitalis purpurea Dalmatian Series (foxglove)

Erigeron karvinskianus (Mexican fleabane)

Euphorbia hypericifolia 'Glitz'

Salvia 'Snow Cushion'

1 Soak the rootballs of the plants in water for half an hour, or until they are wet through. If your planter has holes in the base, line it with a piece of plastic sheeting to prevent the potting mix from falling through. Push the sheeting into the corners.

2 To stop potting mix from falling through the holes in the sides of the planter, as well as to add a decorative touch, line the planter with moss. Start at the bottom of the planter and work upward.

3 Add scoops of potting mix as you line the planter with moss— this will help to hold the moss in place. You may need to hold the moss with one hand and add potting mix with the other, so that the moss does not fall away from the sides.

4 Continue adding moss and potting mix in this way until all four sides of the planter are covered with moss. Bank up the potting mix against the moss, leaving room in the planter for the plants.

5 Take the grasses out of their pots first, loosening the roots a little to encourage them to grow when they are planted. Plant them on either side of the planter.

6 Plant the astrantia next, positioning it in the center of the planter.

7 Plant the other larger plants, adding or taking away potting mix as required, so that the tops of the plants' rootballs are level.

8 Take the small plants out of their pots and tuck them in between the larger plants, trailing them over the edge of the planter.

9 Add more potting mix to the planter to fill in any holes, and level the surface.

10 Add small pieces of moss around the plants, if you wish, to cover the potting mix, although you may not need to do this if the plants are quite tightly packed in. Water the planter and let it drain.

cottage garden in a tub

If you love the look of cottage gardens, don't let a lack of gardening space stop you from planting one of your own. Cramming a simple, old, galvanized-metal washing tub with summer-flowering plants will provide you with a beautiful floral planter.

YOU WILL NEED

Galvanized-metal tub

Hammer and heavy-duty nail (optional)

Drainage crocks

Potting mix

Plants:

Leucanthemum vulgare 'Filigran' (ox-eye daisy)

2 *Lupinus* 'Camelot Rose'

Persicaria bistorta subsp. *carnea* (bistort)

Salvia 'Clotted Cream'

1 Soak the rootballs of all the plants in water for at least 20 minutes, or until they are thoroughly wet. Use the hammer and sturdy nail to make holes in the bottom of the tub if it doesn't have any already (see page 8). Cover the holes with drainage crocks so that they do not become blocked with potting mix.

2 Half-fill the tub with potting mix and level the surface. Take the leucanthemum from its pot first and plant it toward the back of the tub. Add or remove some potting mix so that the top of the plant's rootball is sitting a couple of inches below the rim of the tub.

3 Next, take the salvia from its pot and plant it in front of the leucanthemum, toward the left-hand side of the tub. Plant the persicaria in the same way, but this time on the other side of the tub. Again, add or remove potting mix, as necessary.

4 Finally, add the lupins to the tub, positioning them between the other plants. Add more potting mix to fill in any gaps and level the surface, making sure there are no air pockets. Water the tub and leave to drain.

AFTERCARE

This cottage-garden planter
will look lovely and continue
to bloom for several months in
summer with a regular routine
of deadheading and feeding
(see page 10).

Chapter 3
EDIBLE PLANTS

blueberries in a tub

Blueberries are surprisingly pretty plants and have the added benefit of providing delicious fruit in the summer. They prefer acidic soil, so plant them in an ericaceous potting mix to ensure a healthy plant, and feed weekly during the growing season to encourage a plentiful supply of flowers and berries. Add flowering plants, such as scabious and nemesia, to create a planter that is both charming and practical.

YOU WILL NEED

Large galvanized-metal tub

Drainage crocks

Ericaceous potting mix

Plants:

3 *Nemesia* Myrtille

3 *Scabiosa* 'Pink Mist' (scabious)

Vaccinium corymbosum (blueberry)

1 Soak the rootballs of the plants for about 20 minutes until they are thoroughly wet. Make sure the tub has drainage holes in the bottom. (See page 8 for guidance on adding holes if the tub does not have any.) Cover the holes with drainage crocks so they don't become blocked with potting mix.

2 Half-fill the tub with potting mix, leveling it slightly and making sure that there are no air pockets.

AFTERCARE

Blueberries are lime-hating plants that need soil with a pH of less than 5.5 (and so require ericaceous potting mix). If possible, collect rainwater for watering the blueberry bush, as tap water will raise the pH of the mix.

3 Take the blueberry out of its pot and position it centrally toward the back of the tub. The surface of the plant's rootball should sit a couple of inches below the rim of the tub. Add or take away potting mix to adjust the level as necessary.

4 Take the scabious out of their pots, loosening the roots slightly if they are particularly pot-bound. This will encourage the roots to spread out in their new position.

5 Plant the scabious around the front of the tub, leaving gaps for the nemesia. Again, make sure that the surface of the potting mix around the scabious is level with that of the blueberry.

6 Plant the nemesia in the tub in the same way, checking the arrangement and rearranging the plants a little until you are happy with the final positioning.

7 Take handfuls of potting mix and fill in the gaps around the plants, making sure there are no air pockets. Level the surface of the potting mix so that it is nice and even. Water the tub well.

strawberries in rusty troughs

I love the idea of having containers such as these troughs on a table—not only do they contain edible plants, but they are beautiful to look at too. Picking strawberries when entertaining is a real treat, while adding herbs and edible flowers, such as violas, makes these troughs pretty as well as practical. Try herbs such as basil and parsley, which grow well in containers and are also delicious.

YOU WILL NEED

Metal troughs

Hammer and heavy-duty nail (optional)

Drainage crocks

Potting mix

Plants (for one trough):

3 *Fragaria* × *ananassa* 'Cambridge Favourite' and *F.* × *ananassa* 'Symphony' (strawberry)

1 *Thymus* 'Coccineus Major' or *T.* 'Silver Posie' (thyme)

2 *Viola* 'Huntercombe Purple'

1 Soak the rootballs of the plants in water for about 10 minutes. Use the hammer and nail to make holes in the base of the trough if it does not have any already, to provide adequate drainage.

2 Turn the trough over and cover the base with drainage crocks to prevent the holes from getting blocked with potting mix.

3 Half-fill the trough with potting mix and level the surface a little.

4 Take a strawberry plant from its pot and loosen the rootball a little. Plant the strawberry in the trough, firming in the potting mix to keep it in place. Plant the other two strawberry plants in the trough, spacing them out evenly.

5 Plant the two violas in the trough in the same way.

6 Remove the thyme plants from their pots and add them to the trough between the other plants. Sprinkle more potting mix around the plants to fill in any gaps and press the potting mix down a little. Plant up as many troughs as you need for your table. Water the troughs and leave to drain.

AFTERCARE

Check the potting mix regularly, keeping it moist, rather than very wet. In the growing season, give the strawberry plants a tomato fertilizer to promote good fruits. For the tastiest strawberries, try to harvest during the warmest part of the day.

salad baskets

Salad leaves are so easy to grow and can be cultivated in a very small space—I think everyone should grow them! These baskets make perfect containers since they provide lots of drainage and can be moved to a sunny spot in the garden or placed on a table for a pick-your-own salad.

YOU WILL NEED

Wire baskets

Moss (available from florists and garden centers)

Potting mix

A selection of salad seedlings:

Brassica juncea 'Red Giant' (mustard)

Brassica rapa subsp. *chinensis* (bok/pak choi)

Latuca sativa 'Red Batavia' and *L. sativa* 'Red Salad Bowl' (red-leaved lettuce)

Lycoperscion esculentum 'Heartbreaker' (F1 tomato)

Ocimum basilicum var. *purpurascens* 'Dark Opal' (purple basil)

Rumex acetosa (sorrel)

Rumex sanguineus (red-veined sorrel)

1 Line the base of the basket with moss to hold the potting mix in place.

2 Press pieces of moss against the sides of the basket and add scoops of potting mix to hold the moss in position.

3 Continue to line the basket with moss, overlapping the pieces of moss slightly so there are no gaps.

4 Fill the basket with potting mix and then level it off.

5 Soak the rootball of the tomato plant in water and remove it from its pot. Plant the tomato in the middle of the basket, sinking it into the potting mix so that the top of the rootball is covered with potting mix.

6 Carefully take the first salad seedlings from their tray and plant a few of them at the front of the basket, positioning them an inch or so apart.

7 Plant more seedlings, placing them to one side of the tomato.

8 Plant other seedlings in the remaining spaces. Plant up the other baskets with more salad seedlings. Give the baskets a good water and leave to drain.

AFTERCARE

Pick the salad leaves as required, adding more seedlings if necessary. Water the baskets consistently, as letting them dry out and then soaking them can cause the tomatoes to split. Support the tomato plant with twigs as it grows.

herbs in vintage containers

Herbs are perfect plants for containers because they look beautiful, are easy to grow, and provide delicious flavors for you to use in cooking for months on end. To create a little herb bed when you don't have a garden, collect some old cans (tins) and bowls from secondhand markets and tabletop sales. Group the containers in a pleasing arrangement and then plant them with a range of herbs you like and enjoy.

YOU WILL NEED

Selection of vintage cans
(tins) and bowls in similar or
contrasting colors

Hammer and heavy-duty nail

Drainage crocks

Gravel

Potting mix

PLANTS:

Lavandula 'Pretty Polly'
(lavender)

Origanum vulgare (oregano/
wild marjoram)

Rosmarinus officinalis
(rosemary)

Salvia officinalis 'Purpurascens'
(purple sage)

Thymus 'Golden Queen'
(lemon thyme)

Thymus 'Silver Queen' (thyme)

1 Make holes in the base of
all the containers using the
hammer and large nail. This will
help improve drainage. (If the
containers already have holes,
then omit this step.)

2 Turn the first container the right
way up and cover the holes with
drainage crocks, so that it will
drain well and prevent the herbs
from becoming waterlogged.

3 Add a layer of gravel (about
½in/1cm deep) to the base of
the container. Again, this will help
with drainage.

4 Fill the container about one-third full with potting mix and level the surface.

5 Soak the rootballs of the plants in water until they are thoroughly wet and take them out of their pots. Place the oregano toward one side of the container, ensuring that the surface of the plant's rootball is sitting below the rim.

6 Plant the lavender next to the oregano, checking the level of the plant as before.

7 Fill all around both plants with more potting mix so they sit securely in place, and press down firmly.

8 Add gravel to the surface of the potting mix to help keep the mix moist and also to finish off the look of the container beautifully.

9 Plant up the remainder of the containers with the other herbs. Water the containers carefully and allow them to drain.

AFTERCARE

Check the potting mix in the herb containers regularly and ensure that it is kept moist, but not too wet. Use a general-purpose fertilizer every few weeks to encourage lots of bushy growth.

micro-green tower

Eating micro-greens is very popular at the moment and they are surprisingly easy to grow. The idea involves growing seedlings—which are harvested when they are still small—and then adding them to salads, where their intense flavors can be enjoyed. You can, of course, grow micro-greens in flat trays, which will provide you with ample seedlings, but this towering planter is a fun way to grow them and would make a lovely centerpiece for an al fresco lunch. Just provide a pair of scissors and your guests can help themselves.

YOU WILL NEED

4 metal jello (jelly) molds or bowls in different sizes

Potting mix

A selection of seeds, such as:

Peas, radish, basil, carrots, spinach, and arugula (rocket)

1 Take the largest bowl or mold and fill it with potting mix, breaking up any clumps.

2 Use your hands to flatten down the potting mix, so that it is quite compacted. This will create a level surface for the next bowl or mold to sit on.

3 Place the second largest bowl or mold in the center of the first one. Fill the second bowl or mold with potting mix, again pressing it down firmly in order to compact the surface.

4 Put the third largest bowl or mold on top of the second one, fill with potting mix as before, and then finish with the smallest bowl or mold at the top of the tower. Again, fill this last bowl or mold with potting mix.

5 Sprinkle seeds onto the surface of the potting mix in the top bowl or mold (I used peas here). The seeds should be sown close together, so that you will get a dense planting of lush seedlings.

6 Sprinkle more seeds onto the potting mix in the other layers of the tower (here, I used radish and another type of pea), again sowing them much closer together than you would normally.

7 Water all the seeds well. Keep the potting mix damp and position the tower by a warm window.

AFTERCARE

The seeds will take one to two weeks to germinate. The seedlings can be cut when they are very short, or left to grow a little if you would like longer shoots. Cut the sprouts a little above the potting mix.

berries in an urn

Growing plants that produce fruits is very satisfying and even more so when the plants look beautiful too. This boysenberry has the most enormous, fat, juicy berries with lovely leaves that turn from green to pink, orange, and yellow, so providing interest in the garden for months. Choose a container that has plenty of room for root growth, adding a pretty floral lychnis with its delicate pompom flowers to create a really lovely planter.

YOU WILL NEED

Metal urn

Hammer and heavy-duty nail (optional)

Drainage crocks

Gravel

Potting mix

Plants:

Lychnis flos-cuculi 'Jenny' (ragged robin)

Rubus ursinus × *idaeus* (boysenberry)

1 Soak both of the plants' rootballs in water for about 20 minutes, or until they are soaked through. Use the hammer and nail to make holes in the bottom of the urn, if it does not have any already (see page 8). Cover the holes with crocks to aid drainage.

2 Put a layer of gravel in the bottom of the urn, which will also help to improve drainage.

3 Half-fill the urn with potting mix and spread it into an even layer.

4 Take the boysenberry from its pot and loosen the roots slightly to encourage them to grow out. Plant the boysenberry toward the back of the urn, so that the top of its rootball is at least an inch below the rim.

5 Take the lychnis from its pot and then plant it in front of the boysenberry.

6 Fill the urn with more potting mix, pressing down to firm it and hold the plants in place. Water the urn and allow it to drain.

AFTERCARE

Keep the potting mix damp and feed with a general-purpose fertilizer (see page 10) in the spring and fall (autumn). Prune the boysenberry's branches after it has fruited and it will live quite happily in its container.

Chapter 4
TABLETOP

spring stool planter

Transform a simple painted wooden stool or side table into a stylish planter for spring, creating a cheap and charming garden display. As this container does not have any drainage holes, keep a check on the potting mix to make sure that it does not become too waterlogged in very wet weather. Move to a sheltered spot to dry out if necessary.

YOU WILL NEED

Old wooden stool or side table

Rectangular pieces of wood, for making the box (the exact dimensions will depend on the size of your stool or table)

Long screws and a screwdriver and/or electric drill

Black plastic sheeting

Staple gun

Potting mix

Plants:

Clematis marmoraria (marbled clematis)

Fritillaria meleagris (snake's head fritillary)

Pulsatilla vulgaris 'Alba' and *P. vulgaris* 'Eva Constance' (pasque flower)

Saxifraga Alpino Early Pink Heart, *S.* 'Peter Pan,' and *S.* 'Touran Neon Rose' (saxifrage)

3 *Tulipa* 'Queen of Night' (tulip)

1 Measure and cut four pieces of wood so you have two long pieces and two short pieces to make a rectangular box for the top of the stool. Make the box by screwing the long pieces to the short pieces (pre-drilling the holes first, if necessary, with an electric drill) and screw the box securely to the stool. (Again, pre-drill holes first using the electric drill.)

2 Cut a piece of plastic sheeting to fit inside and line the box, fixing it into place using the staple gun at intervals around the top. This will protect the wood so that it does not suffer water damage.

3 Half-fill the box with potting mix and level out the surface so that it is nice and even.

4 Take the tulips from their pots and place them toward the back of the box to one side. Scoop up some of the surrounding potting mix to hold them in place.

5 Soak the rootballs of the other plants in water until they are soaking wet. Take the pulsatillas from their pots and plant them in the box. Plant the fritillary in the back corner of the box.

6 Plant one of the saxifrages in a corner of the front of the box so that it trails a little over the edge.

7

8

7 Position another saxifrage in the other corner of the box and then the last saxifrage at the front of the box. Squeeze the clematis in between these two saxifrages.

8 Add more potting mix around the plants to fill any holes, and level the surface. The box should look packed with plants. Water the box so that the potting mix is moist, but not too wet.

small table planter with yellow flowers

I am not a big fan of yellow flowers in general, but these striking coreopsis looked so good against the dark gray that I was won over. Search for an old wooden tray and small table at secondhand stores or markets, and then paint both in the same color to create a very stylish planter. Deep trays work better for this project because you can plant them up without disturbing the plants' roots too much.

YOU WILL NEED

Small table

Tray large enough to fit on top of the table

Electric drill

Screwdriver and screws

Scissors

Black plastic sheeting or an old trash can (bin) liner

Staple gun

Potting mix

Plants:

3 *Coreopsis grandiflora* 'Early Sunrise' (tickseed)

1 *Geum* 'Totally Tangerine' (avens)

3 *Hedera helix* (ivy)

AFTERCARE

Water the planter as necessary, but try to avoid overwatering. Deadhead the flowers regularly to keep the planter looking good and to stimulate the production of more flowers.

1 Soak the rootballs of all the plants in water for about 20 minutes. Drill four holes in the base of the tray and use the screwdriver to screw it into position on top of the table.

2 Cut a piece of plastic sheeting to fit inside the tray and fix it in place with the staple gun, pushing it neatly into the corners. Make sure the plastic sheeting cannot be seen over the top of the tray.

3 Add some potting mix to the tray and level it off a little.

4 Take the geum out of its pot first, loosen the potting mix slightly around the roots, and plant it at the back of the tray.

5 Plant the coreopsis in the same way, removing excess potting mix from the roots if you can.

6 Plant the ivy at the front of the tray and add more potting mix to fill in any gaps around the plants. Water the tray, making sure that you do not overwater because the plants will not like sitting in very wet potting mix.

tiny fairy garden

This wide, shallow metal tray is the perfect container for a pretty fairy garden. Choose low-growing plants with small-scale leaves to create a border around the edge, and trail wild strawberries and Australian ivy over the wire arch. Finish the tray with cushion moss to create a garden that any fairy would be delighted to use.

YOU WILL NEED

Large, shallow tray

Hammer and heavy-duty nail

Drainage crocks

Gravel

Potting mix

Cushion moss (available from florists and garden centers)

Piece of chicken wire, approximately 24 x 1½ in (60 x 4cm)

2 lengths of flexible wire, to hold the arch in place

Tiny pot planted with moss, to sit on the chair (optional)

To make the fairy chair:

Twigs

Hand pruners (secateurs)

Hot glue gun and glue sticks

Plants:

Acaena microphylla 'Copper Carpet' (New Zealand burr)

Aethionema 'Warley Rose' (stone cress)

Erigeron karvinskianus (Mexican fleabane)

Fragaria vesca (wild strawberry)

Lobularia maritima (sweet alyssum)

Muehlenbeckia complexa (Australian ivy)

Sedum polytrichoides 'Chocolate Ball' (stonecrop)

Sedum spathulifolium (spoon-leaved stonecrop)

Thymus serpyllum var. *albus* and *T. serpyllum* 'Annie Hall' (creeping thyme)

1 Soak the rootballs of all the plants in water until they are wet through. To create adequate drainage, make holes all over the base of the tray using the hammer and sturdy nail.

2 Turn the tray over and cover the holes in the base with a few drainage crocks to help keep them clear of potting mix.

3 Pour gravel into the tray to cover the base and help with drainage. Half-fill the tray with potting mix and level off.

4 Take the erigeron from its pot first and plant it toward the side of the tray, trailing the foliage over the edge slightly.

5 Plant the sedum, thyme, acaena, lobularia, and aethionema around the edge of the tray in the same way.

6 Plant the wild strawberry in the place where the wire arch will be situated. Plant a piece of muehlenbeckia near the strawberry plant, so that it will trail over the other side of the arch.

7 Take the cushion moss and use it to cover the bare potting mix. Try to keep the moss in big pieces, but break off smaller bits to fit around the edges. Push the moss down onto the potting mix, butting each piece against the other.

8 Take the piece of chicken wire and bend it into an arch shape. Push the arch into the moss and fasten it in position with a couple of U-shaped pieces of wire pushed down through the base into the moss.

9 Train the strawberry and muehlenbeckia over the tiny arch, gently pushing the leaves through the chicken wire to keep the plants in place. Position the fairy chair in front of the arch (see *To make the fairy chair*, below) and add a little planted pot, if you wish.

TO MAKE THE FAIRY CHAIR

1 Cut two twigs, 6in (15cm) long, and place them vertically on the table. Cut six more twigs, this time measuring 3in (8cm). Place one of these twigs on either side of the long twigs, so all the twigs are parallel. Lay the other short twigs horizontally between the long twigs. Glue the twigs together to make the two chair sides.

2 Cut another eight or more twigs, again 3in (8cm) in length, and glue them to both sides of the chair to hold the sides together and so make the seat.

3 Cut 12 or so more twigs. Glue two twigs across the front and back of the chair at the base. Glue two more twigs in a cross at the bottom of the chair. Glue a further three twigs horizontally across the back of the chair and, finally, four or so more twigs vertically to create a backrest.

copper bowl

This old copper bowl came from a junk store. I was tempted to polish it, but then decided to keep its beautiful, dull patina instead and team it with a selection of flowers and foliage that really enhances the copper color.

YOU WILL NEED

Copper bowl

Hammer and heavy-duty nail (optional)

Gravel

Potting mix

Plants:

Cosmos atrosanguineus (chocolate cosmos)

Dryopteris erythrosora (Japanese shield fern)

Nicotiana alata Starmaker Series 'Lime/Purple Bicolor' (tobacco plant)

Oxalis triangularis (purple shamrock)

Saxifraga 'Esther' (encrusted saxifrage)

Sedum spurium 'Fuldaglut' (Caucasian stonecrop)

Solenostemon 'Chocolate Splash' (painted nettle)

1 Soak the rootballs of all the plants in water for about 20 minutes, or until they are wet through. Use the hammer and nail to make holes in the bottom of the bowl if it does not have them already (see page 8). Put a few handfuls of gravel in the bottom of the bowl to help with drainage. Half-fill the bowl with potting mix, spreading it out evenly.

2 Take the cosmos out of its pot first and plant it in the bowl toward the back edge.

3 Take the other plants from their pots and plant them in the bowl, positioning the taller plants in the middle with the smaller plants around them.

4 Trail the sedum and oxalis over the edge of the bowl. Add or take away potting mix at the bottom of the bowl, as necessary, so that the tops of the plants' rootballs are all sitting at a similar level. Add more potting mix to fill in any gaps between the plants. Press on the potting mix to firm it down and hold all the plants in place. Water and leave to drain.

rose garden

These pale blue enamel tubs set off the pretty pink of the miniature roses beautifully and make a stunning centerpiece for a table setting. Using a smaller tub on top of a larger one creates a tiered effect, adding height and more planting room for a real show-stopper of a container. To make the idea even more appealing, miniature roses can often be bought cheaply from stores and florists, making it an economical tabletop garden, too.

YOU WILL NEED

2 enamel tubs (one smaller than the other)

Hammer and heavy-duty nail (optional)

Drainage crocks (optional)

Potting mix

Small plastic plant pot (for the smaller tub to sit on)

Plants:

4 *Hedera helix* (ivy)

6 pink miniature roses (*Rosa*)

1 If the planter is for a one-off special occasion, you won't need to make drainage holes in the tubs (especially if it is for a table centerpiece). However, if it is to be a long-term planter, then make holes in the bottom of both tubs using the hammer and sturdy nail.

2 Put a few drainage crocks in the bottom of the tubs, if you have made drainage holes. (This isn't necessary if you are using the planter as a short-term display and have not added any holes.)

3 Half-fill the smaller tub with potting mix. Soak the plants' rootballs in water for a few minutes and allow them to drain slightly so that they are not dripping wet. Plant two of the roses in the small tub, adding more potting mix around the rootballs.

4 Half-fill the larger tub with potting mix and push the plastic pot upside down into the middle, so that it is filled with potting mix. The top of the pot (i.e. the original base) should be about two-thirds of the way up the height of the tub. Add more potting mix to the large tub, so that it is level with the top of the plastic pot, and press down firmly.

5 Place the smaller tub inside the larger one, positioning it centrally on top of the plastic pot.

6 Take the remaining roses and remove them from their pots. Loosen the potting mix around the roots to make the rootballs a bit smaller and plant them in the larger tub, carefully pushing down the roots into the potting mix. Plant up all the roses in the same way.

7 Take the ivy plants out of their pots and plant them in the larger pot between the roses. Fill in any gaps with more potting mix and press down firmly. Water the tubs.

AFTERCARE

Keep the potting mix damp,
but not too wet (especially if there are
no drainage holes in the tubs). Deadhead
the roses regularly to promote further
flushes of flowers. If the planter is for
a special occasion, use a water spray
bottle to mist the plants slightly before
the big event so that the plants
look fresh and healthy.

trailing flower cans

This hanging arrangement made from reused food cans (tins) is easy to put together and looks very effective. Choose a few trailing plants that will tumble over the edges of the cans, although I think it is nice to get a hint of what lies beneath the plants. Water the cans and then leave them to drain before you hang them up, to avoid getting drips all over your tabletop.

YOU WILL NEED

Clean, empty food cans (tins), with the labels removed

Hammer and heavy-duty nail

Gravel

Potting mix

Galvanized wire

Decorative bird (optional)

Pliers (optional)

Plants:

Calibrachoa 'Callie Apricot' (mini petunia)

Dryopteris erythrosora (Japanese shield fern)

Gazania Daybreak Series (treasure flower)

Lysimachia nummularia 'Aurea' (golden creeping Jenny)

Zinnia 'Profusion Apricot'

AFTERCARE

Small containers can dry out very quickly, especially in warm weather, so check the potting mix and water the cans regularly. Deadhead the plants at the same time to keep them in bloom.

1

2

3

4

5

6

7

8

1 Soak the rootballs of all the plants in water for about 10 minutes, or until they are wet through. Use the hammer and nail to make a hole near the rim of each can (tin), so they can be hung up later.

2 Turn the cans upside down and make a few holes in the base of each to allow for drainage.

3 Add a couple of handfuls of gravel to the bottom of each can to prevent the potting mix from becoming waterlogged.

4 Put handfuls of potting mix in each can, filling them until they are approximately half full.

5 Take the plants out of their pots and remove any excess potting mix to make the rootballs smaller. Place the plants in the cans, adding a little more potting mix (up to an inch or so below the rim) if necessary.

6 Take a length of wire (the length will depend on where you are planning to hang the display) and push the end through the hole in the can. Twist the end of the wire around the length securely so that it will hold the can firmly in place.

7 Make a loop at the other end of the wire and use this to suspend the can with the other planted cans. Vary the lengths of the wires slightly, so that the cans hang in a pleasing arrangement.

8 If you wish, you can add a pretty decoration such as this little bird to the top of the display. You may find a pair of pliers useful for attaching your choice of decoration.

metal containers with blue and white flowers

Grouping containers on a tabletop creates a striking focal point and choosing a simple color combination for the planting gives an effortless charm to the display. Plants in blues and whites always look lovely together, and planting them in a range of containers in different sizes adds further interest.

YOU WILL NEED

Galvanized-metal pails (buckets) and tubs

Hammer and heavy-duty nail

Drainage crocks

Gravel

Potting mix

Plants:

Cerastium tomentosum (snow-in-summer)

Hosta 'Blue Cadet' and *H.* 'Sherborne Swift' (plantain lily)

Lavandula angustifolia 'Imperial Gem' (English lavender)

Origanum vulgare (oregano/wild marjoram)

Parahebe 'Snowclouds'

Salvia nemorosa (Balkan clary)

Salvia officinalis (sage)

Senecio cineraria 'Silver Dust' (silver ragwort)

1 Soak the rootballs of the plants in water for about 20 minutes, or until they are wet through. Make holes in the bottoms of the containers with the hammer and nail to help with drainage.

2 Put drainage crocks in the bottom of each container, so that the drainage holes will not become blocked with potting mix.

AFTERCARE

Water the plants regularly in warm weather and feed with a general-purpose fertilizer (see page 10) every few weeks over the summer to maintain the display.

3 Pour about 1in (2.5cm) of gravel into the bottom of each container to improve the drainage further.

4 Half-fill each container with potting mix and level off to achieve an even surface.

5 Remove the first plant from its pot and carefully loosen the roots a little.

6 Put the plant in the container, adding more potting mix to the bottom if necessary. Plant the remaining containers in the same way. Water the containers well and allow them to drain.

flower chandelier

This pretty planted chandelier could also be made into a table centerpiece. Bedding plants sold in trays are perfect for this planting idea because they have small root systems and are happy to be crammed into confined spaces.

YOU WILL NEED

Sheet moss (available from florists and garden centers)

Wire wreath base, 14in (35cm) in diameter

Potting mix

Fine copper wire

Pliers

Galvanized wire, to suspend the chandelier

A selection of plants, including:

Bacopa (water hyssop)

Brachyscome 'Mini Mauve Delight' (Swan river daisy)

Calibrachoa Cabaret Series (mini petunia)

Lobularia maritima (sweet alyssum)

1 Take pieces of moss and lay them face down in a circular shape on the table. Place the wire wreath base on top of the circle of moss and rearrange the moss if necessary.

2 Sprinkle handfuls of potting mix over the wreath base until it is completely covered.

3 Begin gathering the moss around the wreath base and potting mix, binding them into place with the copper wire as you go. (I used copper wire here, which you might find difficult to see as you work; if so, try using silver wire instead.) Continue binding the moss and potting mix in this way until the whole wreath is covered. Don't worry too much about any gaps in the moss, but make sure that no potting mix can fall out.

4 Soak the rootballs of all the plants in water for a few minutes. Take a plant from its tray and loosen the potting mix a little. Use your finger to make a hole in the moss on top of the wreath and gently push the roots of the plant inside.

5 Continue adding more plants to the wreath in the same way until it is covered and looks lovely and full.

6 Wrap more wire around the wreath between the plants to hold them firmly in place, and finish by twisting the end of the wire around itself. Water the whole wreath and allow to drain before hanging it over a table.

7 To hang the wreath as a chandelier, use the pliers to cut two lengths of wire—the length of these wires will depend on where you plan to hang the chandelier, but they should be double the hanging height, plus about 24in (60cm). Wrap the ends of both wires around the wreath, spacing them out equally, and then twist the ends firmly around the suspending wires, just above the top of the chandelier, to hold them securely in place. Suspend the finished chandelier, perhaps from an arch or pergola.

AFTERCARE

Check the moss and potting mix often, because they will dry out quickly when the weather is warm. Mist the plants regularly in hot weather, watering the chandelier every day if it looks dry.

cream enamel tub with purple and orange

This simple enamel tub helps to set off a jumble of different plants, creating an exuberant display. Positioning taller plants at the back and smaller plants in the front of the tub, and letting trailing plants cascade over the edge, produces a stunning effect, while mixing the colors also creates real interest.

YOU WILL NEED

Large enamel tub

Hammer and heavy-duty nail

Drainage crocks

Potting mix

Plants:

Centaurea montana 'Amethyst in Snow' (cornflower)

Lysimachia nummularia 'Aurea' (golden creeping Jenny)

Orange-red *Osteospermum* (African daisy)

Pelargonium grandiflorum (geranium)

Salvia Love and Wishes (sage)

Sambucus nigra porphyrophylla 'Eva' (black elder)

Tiarella 'Spring Symphony' (foam flower)

Orange *Viola* × *wittrockiana* (pansy)

1 Soak the rootballs of the plants in water for at least 20 minutes, or until they are thoroughly wet. Your tub will need drainage holes, so make some randomly all over the base using the hammer and nail.

2 Line the bottom of the tub with drainage crocks, which will prevent the holes from becoming blocked with potting mix.

3 Half-fill the tub with potting mix and level off to create an even surface.

4 Take the sambucus from its pot and plant it toward one side of the tub, firming down the potting mix.

5 Plant the salvia at the back of the tub, next to the sambucus. Plant the pelargonium in front of the salvia, again firming the potting mix around it.

6 Remove the tiarella from its pot and plant it next to the pelargonium in the same way. Next, plant the centaurea and osteospermum.

7 Plant the lysimachia at the front of the tub, so that its stems trail over the edge, and then tuck in the pansy to one side. Add more potting mix to fill in any gaps and level the surface evenly. Water the tub and allow to drain.

AFTERCARE

The plants in this tub are packed in tightly, so the nutrients in the potting mix will be in demand. Additional feeding every two weeks is recommended, using a general-purpose fertilizer (see page 10).

index

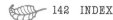

resources

UNITED KINGDOM
Aconbury Sprouts
01981 241155
www.wheatgrass-uk.com
Large selection of seeds suitable for
growing as micro-greens and available
mail order

Alexandra Nurseries
Estate House
Parish Lane
Penge
London SE20 7LJ
020 8778 4145
www.alexandranurseries.co.uk
Lovely selection of plants and vintage
garden accessories

Anthropologie
00 800 0026 8476
www.anthropologie.com
Beautiful homeware and garden
accessories

Columbia Road Flower Market
Columbia Road
London E2 7RG
www.columbiaroad.info
Sunday market with a wonderful
atmosphere selling a wide selection
of fantastic plants

Crocus
01344 578111
www.crocus.co.uk
A wide selection of plants and gardening
accessories available mail order

Heucheraholics
Boldre Nurseries
Southampton Road
Lymington
Hampshire SO41 8ND
01590 670581
www.heucheraholics.co.uk
Nursery specializing in heuchera,
heucherella, and tiarella available mail order

Key Essentials
Pioneer Nursery
Baldock Lane
Willian
Hertfordshire SG6 2AE
01462 675858
www.keyessentials.co.uk
Lovely selection of mail-order air plants,
plus lots of information on care

Mabel and Rose
01993 878861
www.mabelandrose.com
Mail-order company selling beautiful
vintage planters, pails (buckets), and
garden accessories

Petersham Nurseries
Church Lane (off Petersham Road)
Richmond
Surrey TW10 7AG
020 8940 5230
www.petershamnurseries.com
Beautiful plants, pots, and garden furniture

RE
Bishops Yard
Main Street
Corbridge
Northumberland NE45 5LA
01434 634567
www.re-foundobjects.com
Mail-order company selling great garden
accessories and homeware

RHS Wisley
Woking
Surrey GU23 6QB
0845 260 9000
www.rhs.org.uk/gardens/wisley
Huge selection of plants and garden
accessories with a great advice center

Sarah Raven's Kitchen Garden
0345 092 0283
www.sarahraven.com
Beautiful selection of seeds, seedlings,
plants, and gardening accessories available
mail order

Sunbury Antiques Market
Kempton Park Racecourse
Staines Road East
Sunbury-on-Thames
Middlesex TW16 5AQ
01932 230946
www.sunburyantiques.com
A fantastic twice-monthly antique and
bric-a-brac market where you are sure to
find lots of treasure to use in your garden

UNITED STATES AND CANADA
Anthropologie (across USA)
(800) 309-2500
www.anthropologie.com
Beautiful selection of products for the
garden and home

Ben Wolff Pottery
279 Sharon Turnpike
Goshen
Connecticut 06756
(860) 618-2317
www.benwolffpottery.com
Lovely handmade pots and containers

Flora Grubb Gardens
1634 Jerrold Avenue
San Francisco
California 94124
(415) 626-7256
www.floragrubb.com
Planted containers, sky planters, and
wall ornaments

GRDN
103 Hoyt Street
Brooklyn
New York 11217
(718) 797-3628
www.grdnbklyn.com
A beautiful selection of gardening goods

Jayson Home
1885 N Clybourn Avenue
Chicago
Illinois 60614
(800) 472-1885
www.jaysonhome.com
Lovely selection of reclaimed pots
and planters

Potted
3158 Los Feliz Boulevard
Los Angeles
California 90039
(323) 665-3801
www.pottedstore.com
Great selection of planters and
garden accessories

Pottery Barn (across USA)
(888) 779-5176
www.potterybarn.com
Lots of garden accessories and furniture

Pure Modern (online/Canada)
(800) 563-0593
www.puremodern.com
Pots, planters, and garden accessories

West Elm (across USA)
(888) 922-4119
www.westelm.com
Garden containers, accessories,
and furniture

acknowledgments

I have worked on lots of books with Debbie Patterson and every time her enthusiasm for each new project, her calm approach, and her wonderfully creative eye never cease to amaze me. So thank you yet again, Debbie. It was a complete pleasure working on this with you. Love those gorgeous detail shots! Thank you also to Caroline West for such sensitive editing and invaluable support, knowledge, and patience; Luana Gobbo for designing the pages so beautifully; Kerry Lewis for organizing the locations with great efficiency; Anna Galkina for overseeing the whole thing; and, of course, to Cindy Richards for commissioning the book and letting me work with a great team again.

And thank you to my family: Laurie, Gracie, and Betty, without whom I couldn't do any of this. Thank you my loves.